To The Best Nan

1938 - 2023

For information visit: www.amydoslich.com
Written and illustrated by Amy Doslich
Paperback ISBN: 9781961459052
Hardcover ISBN: 9781961459069
Printed in the United States of America
First edition December 2023
4th book in the Hannah Banana and Mary Berry series

Little Girls Love Big

**Written and
Illustrated by
Amy Doslich**

I'm so EXCITED!
Do you know what
day is coming up?
It's Valentine's Day!

Valentine's Day is when you show everyone you love how much you care about them. I love A LOT of people!

My grandpa really LOVES food!
I can bake him some cookies.

Ooooo! I know! She LOVES it when I clean the playroom. I'll pick up all the toys. She will be so happy.

My grandma lives
SUPER far away!
What can I do for her?

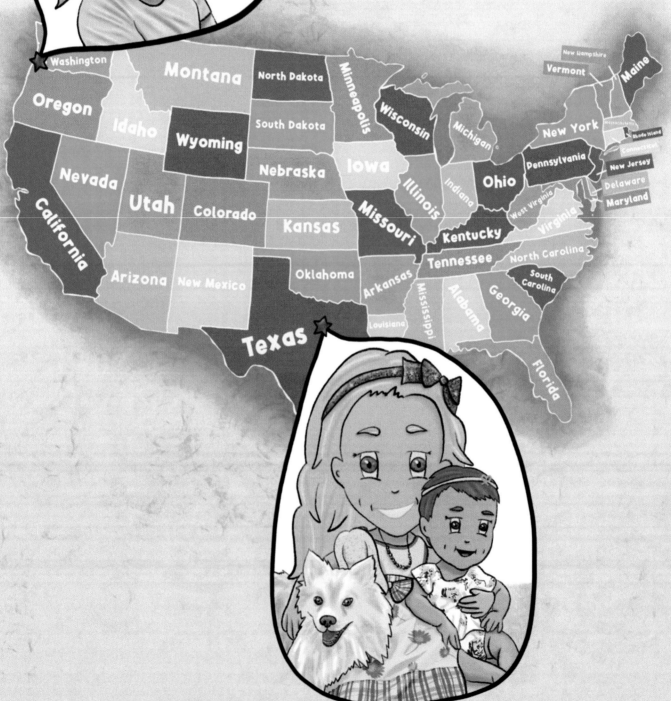

Snowball is the sweetest dog.

He LOVES it when I rub his belly. I'll give him some extra pets today!

Eva and Zoe are twins who live across the
street and are my BEST friends!
They look just alike.

I can't forget to give Pinky a hug!

She LOVES dancing and hugs!

But where is Mary?

Oh WOW!
Mary knows I LOVE bunnies,
so she made me a bunny party!

Check out the below books in the Hannah Banana and Mary Berry series with more books coming soon!

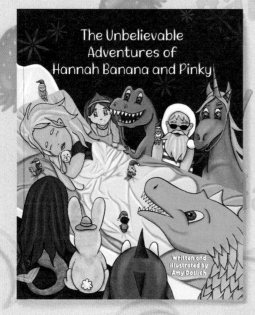

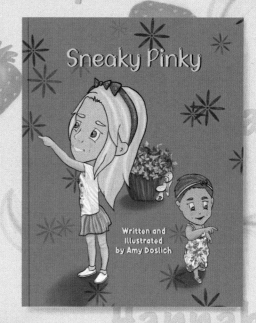

Thank you so much for purchasing this book. I would love to connect with you! Please check out my website to get in touch by scanning the QR code to the right.

I'm so grateful for you spending time reading my book! If you would like to help me and future readers out, please consider leaving a review wherever you purchased this book. I read every single review I receive!

Made in the USA
Las Vegas, NV
11 February 2024

85640877R00019